Canadian Animals
Belugas

Simon Rose

Weigl

Published by Weigl Educational Publishers Limited
6325 10th Street S.E.
T2H 2Z9
Calgary, Alberta

www.weigl.com
Canadian Animals series © 2011
Weigl Educational Publishers Limited

Library and Archives Canada Cataloguing in Publication

Belugas / Simon Rose.
Rose, Simon, 1961-

(Canadian animals)
Includes index.
Issued also in electronic format.
ISBN 978-1-55388-674-7 (bound).–ISBN 978-1-55388-675-4 (pbk.)

1. White whale–Canada–Juvenile literature.
I. Title. II. Series: Canadian animals (Calgary, Alta.)

QL737.C433R67 2010   j599.5'420971   C2009-907379-X
2010a j599.5'420971 C2009-907380-3

Editor
Josh Skapin
Design
Terry Paulhus

Photograph Credits
Every reasonable effort has been made to trace ownership and to obtain permission to reprint copyright material. The publishers would be pleased to have any errors or omissions brought to their attention so that they may be corrected in subsequent printings.

Weigl acknowledges Getty Images as its primary image supplier for this title.

We gratefully acknowledge the financial support of the Government of Canada through the Canada Book Fund for our publishing activities.

Printed in the United States of America in North Mankato, Minnesota
1 2 3 4 5 6 7 8 9 14 13 12 11 10

072010
WEP230610

Contents

Meet the Beluga

Belugas are small, white whales that live in the Arctic Ocean. The beluga's body is stocky with a rounded head. The head has tiny eyes and a small beak. There is an almost square-shaped flipper on each side of the beluga's body. The beluga's tail **flukes** become more curved as the whale gets older.

Belugas have layers of fat called blubber. The blubber can be as thick as 12 centimetres. It helps keep the whale's body warm in the cold Arctic waters where these animals live.

▼ Unlike other whales, belugas do not have a fin on their back. This is so they can swim beneath Arctic ice.

Beluga Facts

- The word *beluga* comes from a Russian word meaning "white." Belugas are sometimes called white whales.

- Baby belugas are called **calves**.

▲ The scientific name for the beluga is *delphinapterus*.

How Belugas Breathe

Belugas are **mammals** that breathe through a hole on their head called a blowhole. The blowhole has a flap made from muscle. The flap opens to let in air and closes to keep out water. When belugas breathe out, a spout of water comes shooting through the blowhole. Water from a beluga's spout can shoot as high as 90 centimetres in the air.

▼ Belugas swim to the surface of the water when they need air.

The front of the beluga's head is called the melon. The melon helps belugas sense sound.

Belugas breathe through their blowhole.

Flippers help belugas steer while swimming.

Belugas have small, dark eyes. They are located behind the corners of their mouth.

Belugas use their teeth for grasping and tearing food.

A Very Special Animal

The beluga's body is made for living in the ocean. On the beluga's forehead is a large fatty lump called a melon. This lump is quite flexible. It allows a beluga to change the **expression** on its face.

Belugas are the only whales that have a neck. This neck allows them to turn their head in different directions.

▶ Belugas make faces to communicate with other whales.

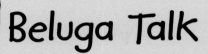

Beluga Talk

- Belugas make many sounds. They can whistle, click, and squeak. These sounds are used to communicate with other belugas and to find **prey**. Belugas often bellow, or call loudly, to each other.

- The beluga makes high-pitched sounds that echo off objects. The echoes let belugas make a picture of their surroundings. This is called **echolocation**.

▲ The beluga is sometimes called the "canary of the sea." Canaries are known for singing, and belugas often make noises that sound like they are singing.

How Belugas Eat

Belugas eat about 100 different kinds of animals. They feed on fish, such as cod, herring and flounder. They also eat squid, octopus, crabs, shrimp, snails, and sandworms.

Belugas often hunt in shallow water for their prey. They can dive more than 600 metres underwater, looking for food.

▼ Adult belugas eat up to 27 kilograms of food each day.

What a Meal!

Belugas hunt schools of fish. They will herd the fish into shallow water before attacking.

▲ Scientists think the beluga can use its mouth to suck like a vacuum. The suction from the beluga's mouth helps it catch prey on the ocean floor.

Where Belugas Live

In Canada, belugas can be found in Hudson Bay and the Gulf of St. Lawrence. Another home for belugas is the Bering and Beaufort Seas, near Alaska. They also live in the Arctic Ocean and the nearby Sea of Okhotsk, which borders Japan and Russia. In spring and winter, most belugas are found in ice-covered regions. Belugas live in coastal areas in summer and fall.

▼ About 9,000 belugas live on the west side of Hudson Bay. A smaller population lives on the east side of Hudson Bay.

Beluga Range

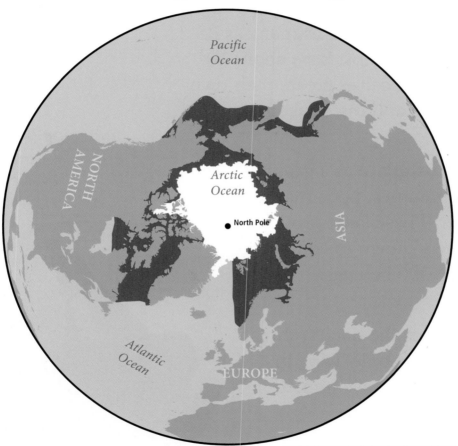

Pacific
Ocean

NORTH
AMERICA

Arctic
Ocean

• North Pole

ASIA

Atlantic
Ocean

EUROPE

 Known Beluga Range

Friends and Enemies

Belugas live together in groups called **pods**. Pods can have as many as 25 members, but most have about 10. Mothers and calves create their own pod during **calving season**.

Belugas **migrate** as a group, and, sometimes, pods may join together. These large groups have been known to contain up to 10,000 belugas.

Humans are the biggest threat to belugas. People living in Arctic regions have hunted belugas for centuries.

▼ In nature, the killer whale is a main enemy of belugas.

Comparing Speed

Belugas are known to be slow swimmers. They swim between 3 and 9 kilometres per hour. This can be a problem for belugas when trying to escape predators, such as the polar bear.

▲ Polar bears can swim up to 10 kilometres per hour.

Growing Up

Female belugas have calves every two to three years. Calves are most often born between May and July.

When belugas are born, they weigh about 80 kilograms and are about 1.5 metres long. The calves know they need to swim to the surface to breathe air. Their mothers help them reach the surface.

▼ Mothers and calves form the beluga's closest bond.

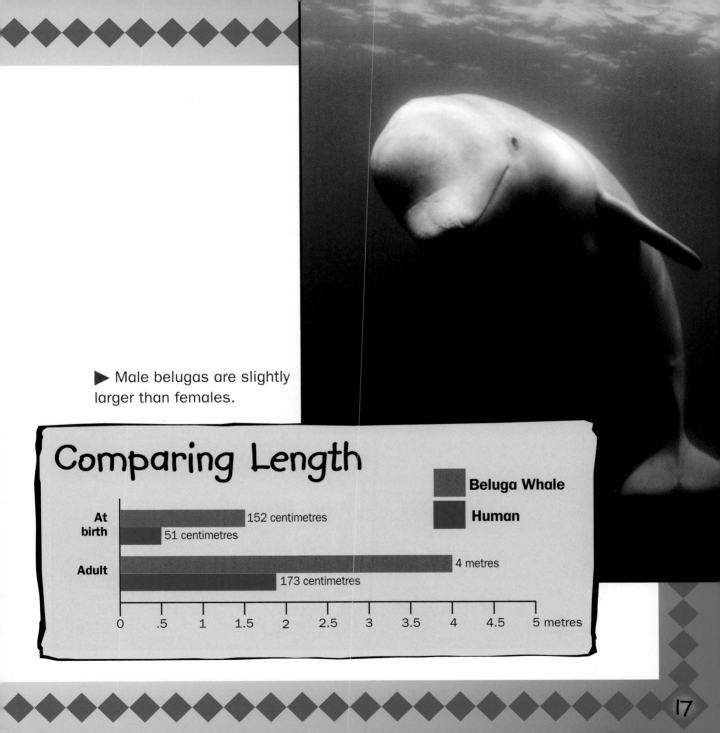

▶ Male belugas are slightly larger than females.

Comparing Length

■ **Beluga Whale**
■ **Human**

At birth
152 centimetres
51 centimetres

Adult
4 metres
173 centimetres

0   .5   1   1.5   2   2.5   3   3.5   4   4.5   5 metres

Under Threat

Belugas are hunted for food. It has caused the beluga population to decrease. Belugas are now protected from people hunting them to sell their meat.

▼ Currently, there are between 60,000 and 80,000 belugas in the world.

What Do You Think?

Human activity can destroy a beluga's **habitat**. A beluga's home is affected by pollution from industries. Some industries make waste that is dumped into the ocean. Should industries be allowed to dump waste near beluga habitats? How can people work to decrease pollution?

▲ Oil spills are one way water can become polluted.

Myths and Legends

People have been telling stories about whales for hundreds of years. Some people have written songs about whales. Children's music performer Raffi sings a well-known song called "Baby Beluga." Raffi wrote the song after seeing a baby beluga in the Vancouver Aquarium.

▲ The Bible tells the story of a man named Jonah who was swallowed by a whale.

The story of a beluga named Keiko tells how the first human war started. Keiko married a woman who later gave birth to a small whale. The woman kept the baby whale in a cup until it grew too large and had to be set free. The baby whale was hunted for food. This upset the baby whale's parents, and they started a war to seek revenge.

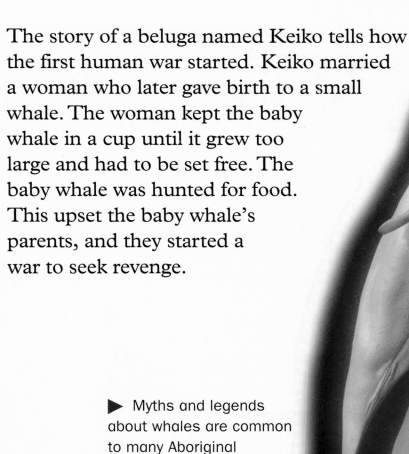

▶ Myths and legends about whales are common to many Aboriginal Peoples who live in the Arctic.

Quiz

1. What is a baby beluga called?
   (a) **cub** (b) **calf** (c) **pup**

2. Which animal is a beluga's enemy?
   (a) **killer whale** (b) **dolphin** (c) **penguin**

3. What is a group of belugas called?
   (a) **school** (b) **pod** (c) **herd**

4. What does a beluga use to breathe?
   (a) **blowhole** (b) **blubber** (c) **flipper**

5. What type of animal is a beluga?
   (a) **fish** (b) **reptile** (c) **mammal**

Answers:
1. (b) A baby beluga is called a calf.
2. (a) The killer whale is an enemy to the beluga.
3. (b) A group of belugas is called a pod.
4. (a) Belugas use a blowhole to breathe.
5. (c) The beluga is a mammal.

Find out More

To find out more about belugas, you can write to these organizations or visit their websites.

Vancouver Aquarium
P.O. Box 3232
Vancouver, British Columbia
V6B 3X8
www.vanaqua.org

The Nature Conservancy of Canada
36 Eglinton Avenue West, Suite 400
Toronto, Ontario
M4R 1A1
www.natureconservancy.ca

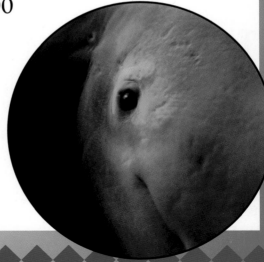

Words to Know

calves
baby or young whales

calving season
the time of year when belugas are born

echolocation
the process of locating objects by using high-pitched sounds that bounce off an object and return to the sender as an echo

expression
gestures created by face muscles

flukes
a pair of horizontal tail fins that the beluga uses to swim

habitat
the natural environment where animals and plants live

mammals
animals that give birth to live young and feed milk to their offspring

migrate
to move from place to place depending on the season

pods
groups of whales

prey
animals that are hunted for food

Index